# United States Presidents

## Harry S. Truman

Paul Joseph
ABDO Publishing Company

# visit us at
# www.abdopub.com

Published by Abdo Publishing Company 4940 Viking Drive, Edina, Minnesota 55435. Copyright © 1999 by Abdo Consulting Group, Inc. International copyrights reserved in all countries. No part of this book may be reproduced in any form without written permission from the publisher.

Printed in the United States.

Cover and Interior Photo credits:  Peter Arnold, Inc., SuperStock, Archive, Corbis-Bettmann

Contributing editors: Robert Italia, Tamara L. Britton, K. M. Brielmaier
Book design/maps: Patrick Laurel

## Library of Congress Cataloging-in-Publication Data

Joseph, Paul, 1970-
    Harry S. Truman / Paul Joseph.
        p.  cm. -- (United States presidents)
    Includes index.
    Summary:  A biography of the senator from Missouri who became the thirty-third president of the United States in 1945.
    ISBN 1-56239-743-5
    1.  Truman, Harry S., 1884-1972--Juvenile literature.
2. Presidents--United States--Biography--Juvenile literature.
[1. Truman, Harry S., 1884-1972. 2. Presidents.]  I. Title.
II. Series: United States presidents (Edina, Minn.)
E814.J67  1999
973.918'092
[B] --DC21                                     97-46688
                                                  CIP
                                                   AC

# Contents

# Harry S. Truman

*O*n April 12, 1945, Vice President Harry S. Truman was called to the White House. There, Truman learned that President Franklin D. Roosevelt had died. Now, Truman was the thirty-third U.S. president. It was a job he never wanted.

In 1944, President Roosevelt decided to run for a fourth term. Henry Wallace was his vice president. But the **Democrats** felt Wallace would hurt Roosevelt's chances at re-election. They chose Senator Harry Truman to run for vice president.

Truman did not want that job, either. He liked being a senator. Roosevelt and other Democrats pressured Truman. He finally said yes.

Truman became vice president at a difficult time. **World War II** had begun. When he became president, Truman made some of the hardest decisions in world history.

Truman was a farmer from Missouri. He worked hard to serve his state and country. He left the White House as one of the country's most important presidents.

*President Truman in the Oval Office of the White House*

# *Harry S. Truman* (1884-1972)
## Thirty-third President

| | |
|---|---|
| BORN: | May 8, 1884 |
| PLACE OF BIRTH: | Lamar, Missouri |
| ANCESTRY: | English, Scots-Irish |
| FATHER: | John Anderson Truman (1851-1914) |
| MOTHER: | Martha Ellen Young Truman (1852-1947) |
| WIFE: | Elizabeth "Bess" Virginia Wallace (1885-1982) |
| CHILDREN: | One girl |
| EDUCATION: | Graduated from Independence High School (1901), Independence, Missouri |
| RELIGION: | Baptist |
| OCCUPATION: | Railroad time keeper, bank clerk, businessman, farmer |
| MILITARY SERVICE: | Missouri National Guard; captain in 129th field artillery |
| POLITICAL PARTY: | Democrat |

OFFICES HELD: County judge for Eastern District of Jackson County, Missouri; presiding judge, Jackson County Court, Missouri; U.S. senator; vice president

AGE AT INAUGURATION: 60

YEARS SERVED: 1945-1949, 1949-1953

VICE PRESIDENT: Alben Barkley (1949-1953)

DIED: December 26, 1972, Kansas City, Missouri, age 88

CAUSE OF DEATH: Heart failure

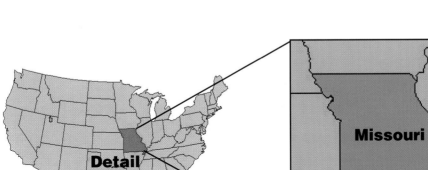

**Birthplace of Harry S. Truman**

# Young Harry

*H*arry S. Truman was born May 8, 1884, in Lamar, Missouri. He was the son of John Anderson Truman, a farmer and cattle trader, and Martha Young Truman.

In 1890, the Truman family moved to Independence, Missouri. There, Harry attended school. When he was nine years old, Harry had to start wearing glasses. His poor eyesight kept him from playing sports.

When Harry was nine, he caught **diphtheria**. He was sick for many months. He could not talk or move his arms and legs. He had to quit school. As he got better, he took lessons at home to keep up. Harry skipped the third grade because he had studied so hard at home.

Harry liked to read and play the piano. Mark Twain was his favorite author. Chopin and Mozart were his favorite **composers**. Harry spent much of his spare time at the Independence library. He read many novels, history books, and encyclopedias. Harry even read the Bible twice before he was 12.

History was Harry's best subject in high school. "I doubt if there was a student in any high school in the country who knew more of the history of the United States than Harry did," said Mrs. Brown, his high school history teacher.

In 1901, Harry applied to the military academy at West Point. He was not accepted because of his poor eyesight. Harry was very smart. But he could not afford college. Harry moved to Kansas City. He worked at a railroad, a bank, and a newspaper.

Harry stayed in Kansas City for five years. Then his father asked Harry to help run the family farm in Grandview, Missouri. Harry worked there for over 10 years.

Harry tried some different business ideas while he was a farmer. He bought a **mineral** mine with his friends. But they lost their money. Later, Harry owned part of an oil company. He gave it up when **World War I** started.

*Harry Truman got his first pair of glasses when he was nine years old.*

# Harry and Bess

*I*n 1917, the United States entered **World War I**. Truman was still a farmer. He was also a member of the Missouri National Guard. In March 1918, Truman went to France as an **artillery** captain. He fought well in several battles.

*Harry and Bess on their wedding day*

Truman married Elizabeth "Bess" Wallace in 1919. They had been childhood sweethearts. On February 17, 1924, the Trumans had their only child. They named her Mary Margaret.

Truman invested in a clothing business in 1920. It made money for two years. Then it failed during a **depression**.

In 1922, Truman decided to work in politics. Thomas Pendergast, a powerful politician, helped Truman's career. Truman became a Jackson County judge.

In 1924, Truman ran for re-election, but lost. "I was broke and out of a job with a family to support," he said. "Thankfully, I had a lot of friends who helped pull me through it until 1926."

For Truman, 1926 was an important year. He was elected to the Jackson County Court. Truman was in charge of government money for construction projects. He did his job well. He became known as an honest politician.

*Truman (left) in his clothing store*

# Senator Truman

*I*n 1934, Truman decided to run for the U.S. Senate. People liked Truman's ideas. With Pendergast's help, Truman was elected.

At first, the other senators did not like Truman. They thought he had won the election because of Thomas Pendergast. But as a senator, Truman worked hard. He soon gained people's respect.

*Senator Truman with Thomas Pendergast*

In 1940, Truman was re-elected. By now, **World War II** had begun. Truman was concerned about government money spent on the war. He wanted to make sure this money was not wasted.

Truman traveled across the nation in his car. He visited factories that made weapons and war supplies. Their careless spending shocked him.

Truman formed the Truman Committee to stop wasteful spending. This group helped the government save billions of dollars. Truman was now one of America's best-known politicians.

*Harry and Bess Truman learn of Harry's win in the U.S. Senate race.*

# *The Making of the Thirty-third United States President*

**1884**
Born May 8 in Lamar, Missouri

**1890**
Moves to Independence, Missouri

**1893**
Gets first pair of glasses

**1901**
Graduates from high school; moves to Kansas City, Missouri

**1920**
Starts a clothing business

**1922**
Business fails; elected Jackson County judge

**1924**
Daughter Mary Margaret born February 17; loses re-election

**1926**
Elected to Jackson County Court

**1945**
April 12, President Roosevelt dies; Truman becomes 33rd U.S. president; WWII ends

**1946**
Strikes cripple the country; shortages in food, housing, and clothing

**1948**
Elected president in a close race

**1950**
Korean War begins; assassination attempt on Truman

**1952**
Dwight D. Eisenhower elected president

## PRESIDENTIAL YEARS

# *Harry S. Truman*

*"The responsibility of the great states is to serve and not to dominate the world."*

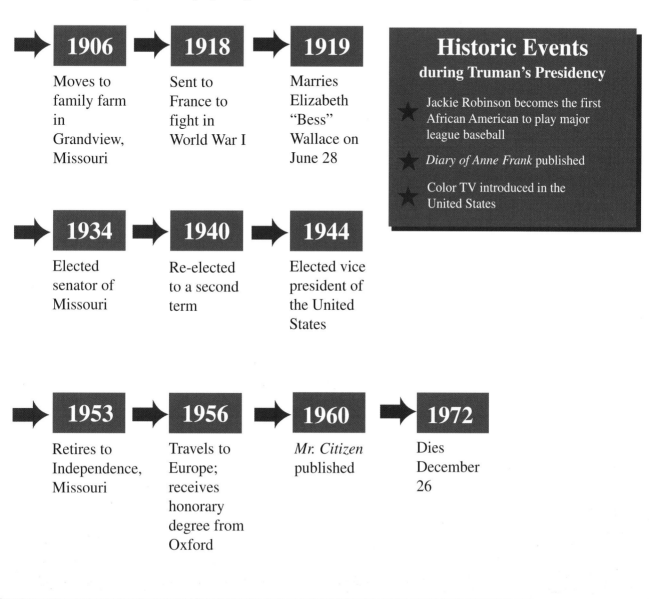

**1906**

Moves to family farm in Grandview, Missouri

**1918**

Sent to France to fight in World War I

**1919**

Marries Elizabeth "Bess" Wallace on June 28

### Historic Events
**during Truman's Presidency**

★ Jackie Robinson becomes the first African American to play major league baseball

★ *Diary of Anne Frank* published

★ Color TV introduced in the United States

**1934**

Elected senator of Missouri

**1940**

Re-elected to a second term

**1944**

Elected vice president of the United States

**1953**

Retires to Independence, Missouri

**1956**

Travels to Europe; receives honorary degree from Oxford

**1960**

*Mr. Citizen* published

**1972**

Dies December 26

# Vice President Truman

*I*n 1944, the **Democrats** chose President Roosevelt to run for a fourth term.  But they wanted a new vice president.

The current vice president, Henry Wallace, had **radical** views.  Another choice, James Byrnes, was too **conservative**.  Democrats feared either choice would hurt Roosevelt's re-election chances.

The Democrats liked Truman's moderate views.  These views appealed to the most voters.  But Truman did not want the job.

Truman was happy in the Senate.  There, he felt he could help the nation.  He feared that he could not accomplish as much in the vice president's job.

*Franklin D. Roosevelt*

*16*

President Roosevelt and **Democratic** leaders pressured Truman. He finally said yes. Roosevelt and Truman won the election. But Truman hoped one day to return to the Senate.

As vice president, Truman made no important decisions. Roosevelt rarely asked for his advice. He met with Truman only twice.

*At a meeting in 1944, the Democrats chose Harry Truman (center) to run for vice president.*

# World War II Ends

*O*n April 12, 1945, President Roosevelt suddenly died. By law, Truman became the U.S. president.

Truman faced a big problem. He was not prepared to be president. And **World War II** was still raging. Truman worried about the number of people dying each day. He promised America a "speedy victory." And he promised to work for world peace.

Two weeks later, Truman learned of a top secret project. It was called the Manhattan Project. The U.S. government was making an **atomic bomb**.

On May 8, 1945, Germany **surrendered**. The war in Europe was over. But in Asia, America was still at war with Japan. Many people were dying every day.

*An atomic bomb explodes over Hiroshima, Japan.*

18

Truman faced one of the hardest decisions in world history. He had to decide whether to use the **atomic bomb** on Japan. One bomb could destroy a city. Truman hoped this power would scare Japan, and force its **surrender**.

Truman warned Japan about the bomb. He said America would use it if Japan did not surrender. Japan refused to stop fighting.

On August 6, 1945, an atomic bomb exploded over Hiroshima, Japan. The city was destroyed. Three days later, another bomb destroyed the city of Nagasaki. On September 2, 1945, Japan surrendered.

*Hiroshima, Japan, after an atomic bomb exploded*

Truman's tough decision took thousands of Japanese lives. But **World War II** was finally over.

After the war, world leaders helped form the United Nations. Countries agreed to work for world peace. Truman approved of the United Nations. America joined in December 1945.

But there was trouble. During the war, the Soviet Union defeated German troops in many European countries. Now, the Soviets controlled these countries. They also controlled half of Germany.

America and its **allies** wanted the Soviet Union to withdraw its troops from Europe. But the Soviets refused to move. America and the Soviet Union remained enemies for almost 50 years. This was called the Cold War. But no military action was ever taken to force the Soviets from Europe.

*Truman receives Japan's surrender papers that officially end World War II.*

20

Truman faced other problems in Europe. **World War II** ruined many countries. Truman feared the Soviet Union would control Greece and Turkey if the two countries did not get help from America. Truman came up with a plan called the Truman Doctrine. It gave Greece and Turkey money to rebuild.

A few months later, the U.S. gave money to rebuild much of Europe. This action was called the Marshall Plan. It was named after its author, U.S. **Secretary of State** George Marshall.

*Much of Europe was in ruins after World War II.*

# The Seven "Hats" of the U.S. President

A president can serve only two terms. Each term lasts four years. This law was passed while Truman was president, so it did not affect him.

A president is elected or re-elected every four years.

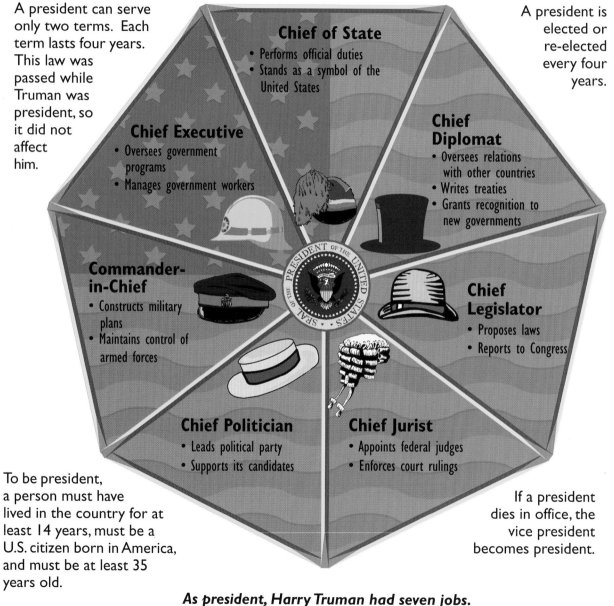

**Chief of State**
- Performs official duties
- Stands as a symbol of the United States

**Chief Diplomat**
- Oversees relations with other countries
- Writes treaties
- Grants recognition to new governments

**Chief Executive**
- Oversees government programs
- Manages government workers

**Commander-in-Chief**
- Constructs military plans
- Maintains control of armed forces

**Chief Legislator**
- Proposes laws
- Reports to Congress

**Chief Politician**
- Leads political party
- Supports its candidates

**Chief Jurist**
- Appoints federal judges
- Enforces court rulings

To be president, a person must have lived in the country for at least 14 years, must be a U.S. citizen born in America, and must be at least 35 years old.

If a president dies in office, the vice president becomes president.

*As president, Harry Truman had seven jobs.*

# The Three Branches of the U.S. Government

Congress is in the Capitol Building in Washington, D.C. It can pass laws and stop the president's veto. Congress also can change the Constitution to stop the president's plans or Supreme Court rulings.

The president lives in the White House in Washington, D.C. He or she can stop (veto) laws passed by Congress, and propose new laws. The president also can choose Supreme Court judges.

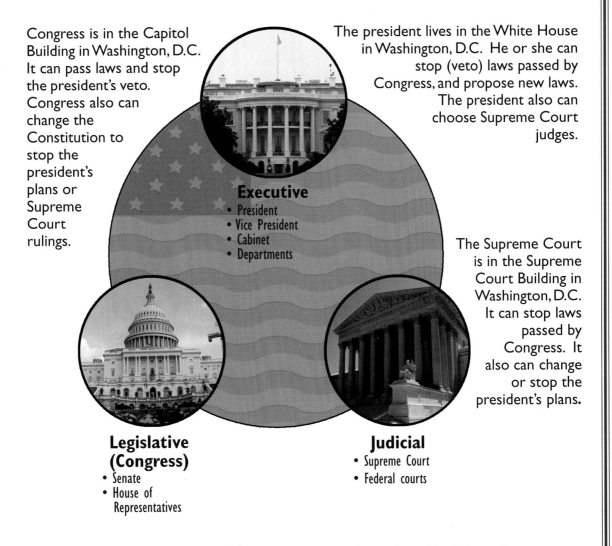

**Executive**
- President
- Vice President
- Cabinet
- Departments

The Supreme Court is in the Supreme Court Building in Washington, D.C. It can stop laws passed by Congress. It also can change or stop the president's plans.

**Legislative (Congress)**
- Senate
- House of Representatives

**Judicial**
- Supreme Court
- Federal courts

*The U.S. Constitution formed three government branches. Each branch has power over the others. So, no single group or person can control the country. The Constitution calls this "separation of powers."*

# Dewey Defeats Truman?

*P*resident Truman also faced problems in America. By January 1946, over a million workers were on strike. They refused to work until they were paid more money. Railroads shut down. Factories closed. It was the worst labor trouble in U.S. history.

Because of the strikes, the **Democrats** did not think Truman could win re-election. Instead, they wanted war hero General Dwight D. Eisenhower to run for president. When Eisenhower refused, the Democrats chose Truman.

The **Republicans** picked New York governor Thomas Dewey to run for president. Many Americans thought Dewey would win the election.

But Truman never quit. He traveled across the nation. He gave more than 300 speeches. Truman blamed the "do-nothing Republican **Congress**" for America's problems. At that time, there were more Republican congressmen than Democrats in Congress. They controlled Congress with their voting power.

The election took place on November 2. Radio reports and newspapers said Truman had lost. The headline on the front page of the *Chicago Daily Tribune* read: "Dewey Defeats Truman."

All the votes were counted the next morning. Truman won the election. It was the biggest political upset in U.S. history.

The **Republican Congress** was shocked. They had hoped to finally put a Republican president in the White House. **Democrat** Franklin Roosevelt had been president from 1933 to 1945. Now, Truman would be president four more years. After that term ended, he could run for re-election.

In 1947, Congress passed an **amendment** to the Constitution. Any future president could only serve two full terms, or a total of 10 years.

*Truman holds up a newspaper printed before all the votes in the 1948 election were counted.*

# Truman Goes Home

*I*n August 1949, the Soviet Union tested an **atomic bomb**. Truman decided America should make more atomic weapons. He did not want the Soviet Union to have more. Then, they might take over more countries. The **arms race** had begun.

In 1950, the Korean War started. North Korea was a **communist** country. It wanted to take over South Korea.

Again, Truman worried about the Soviet Union taking control of more countries. He sent U.S. soldiers to help United Nations forces defend South Korea. Many Americans died in the fighting.

From 1948 to 1952, Truman and his family did not live in the White House. It was being rebuilt. They had to live in Blair House. It was across the street from the White House. On November 1, 1950, Truman survived an **assassination** attempt at Blair House.

In 1951, Truman had trouble with U.S. General Douglas MacArthur. He was a **World War II** hero. He commanded the United Nations forces in the Korean War.

In 1950, two men tried to enter Blair House to kill President Truman. One of the men (A) approached from the left. He was killed (left +) by a police guard.

The other man (B) approached from the right. He was wounded (right +) by another guard. Truman had been napping in a second-floor room (C).

Truman wanted to make peace with North Korea and its powerful **ally**, China. But MacArthur warned China he would attack them. Truman removed MacArthur from his command. As Commander-in-chief, Truman felt he needed to control the U.S. military.

Truman decided not to run for re-election in 1952. Instead, Dwight D. Eisenhower became president. Truman retired to his home in Independence, Missouri.

Truman enjoyed a quiet life with his wife. He wrote his life story, titled *Mr. Citizen.* He traveled to Europe and received an honorary degree from Oxford University. He also helped with the new Harry S. Truman Library in Independence. He died of heart failure on December 26, 1972.

Harry S. Truman was an honest, hard-working man. He became president at one of the most troubled times in U.S. history. He is best remembered for his leadership at the end of **World War II**.

*Harry Truman holds a copy of his book in 1960.*

28

# Fun Facts

- Harry Truman's full middle name is "S." His parents could not decide between "Shippe," in honor of his father's father, or "Solomon," in honor of his mother's father. So they agreed on "S" in honor of both men.

- Truman was the only 20th century president who did not attend college.

- When Harry Truman was sworn in as president, he was so nervous that he had to read the oath of office from a slip of paper.

- By age 14, Harry Truman had read every book in the Independence, Missouri, public library.

- As a boy, Truman got up every morning at 5:00 to practice the piano for two hours before school started. It was a skill he used the rest of his life.

# Glossary

**allies** - countries that agree to help each other in times of need.

**amendment** - a change to the constitution of the United States.

**arms race** - a rivalry between the U.S. and the Soviet Union. Each wanted to have the most atomic weapons.

**artillery** - a division of the army in which large guns are carried on wheels.

**assassination** - when a very important person is killed.

**atomic bomb** - a bomb that uses the energy of an atom. It is thousands of times more powerful than a regular bomb.

**communist** - a system where everything is owned by the government.

**composer** - a person who writes music.

**Congress** - the lawmaking body of the U.S. It is made up of the Senate and the House of Representatives.

**conservative** - a person who opposes change.

**Democrat** - one of the two main political parties in the United States. Democrats are often liberal and believe in more government control.

**depression** - a period of time when prices are high and jobs are hard to find.

**diphtheria** - a disease that causes high fever and sometimes paralysis.

**mineral** - a hard mass such as iron or gold found in the ground.

**radical** - a person who wants quick and major government changes.

**Republican** - one of the two main political parties in the United States. Republicans are often conservative and believe in less government control.

**secretary of state** - a member of the president's cabinet who handles problems with other countries.

**surrender** - to give up.

**World War I** - from 1914 to 1918, America, Great Britain, France, Russia, and their allies fought Germany and its allies.

**World War II** - from 1939 to 1945, America, Great Britain, the Soviet Union, and their allies fought Germany, Italy, Japan, and their allies.

# Internet Sites

**Harry S. Truman Presidential Library and Museum**
http://www.trumanlibrary.org/
Visit the official Web site of the 33rd president, Harry S. Truman. This site has an extensive biography on President Truman along with his speeches, cabinet, photos, and a kid's page.

**Welcome to the White House**
http://www.whitehouse.gov
The official Web site of the White House. After an introduction from the current president of the United States, the site takes you through biographies of each president. Get information on White House history, art in the White House, first ladies, first families, and much more.

**POTUS—Presidents of the United States**
http://www.ipl.org/ref/POTUS/
In this Web site you will find background information, election results, cabinet members, presidency highlights, and some odd facts on each of the presidents. Links to biographies, historical documents, audio and video files, and other presidential sites are also included to enrich this site.

*These sites are subject to change. Go to your favorite search engine and type in United States presidents for more sites.*

# Pass It On

   History enthusiasts: educate readers around the country by passing on information you've learned about presidents or other important people who have changed history. Share your little-known facts and interesting stories. We want to hear from you!
   **To get posted on the ABDO Publishing Company Web site, email us at "History@abdopub.com"**
   **Visit the ABDO Publishing Company Web site at www.abdopub.com**

# Index